MY ADVENTURES
WITH

ABCs

This book was especially written for
Payton Rose Johnson
with love from
Grandma & Aunty Tabitha

April 2010

These picture icons help make activity directions
easy for young learners to follow!

Colour   Write   Circle   Say   Draw   Trace

By Kate Andresen
ISBN 1 875676 25 2

Learning the alphabet is even more fun when you have friends to help you—especially when those friends are Elmo and the Sesame Street gang.

Elmo is ready to learn the Animal Alphabet, from ape to zebra! Can you help Elmo and the others name as many animals as you can, starting with the letter **A** all the way through to **Z**?

Then, have some fun reading and writing the letters of the alphabet and learning about letter partners.

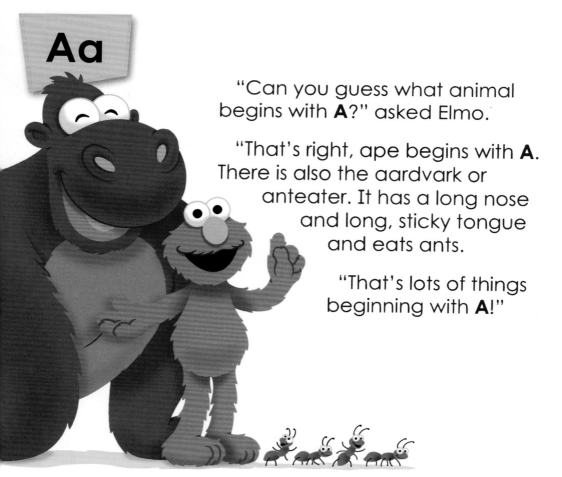

Aa

"Can you guess what animal begins with **A**?" asked Elmo.

"That's right, ape begins with **A**. There is also the aardvark or anteater. It has a long nose and long, sticky tongue and eats ants.

"That's lots of things beginning with **A**!"

Bb

It was Payton Rose's turn to name something beginning with **B**.

"I know," said Payton Rose. "Bear begins with **B**! A bear's favourite meal is honey. And bees make honey. That's two things beginning with **B**!"

Cc

Cookie Monster begins with **C**. Cookie Monster is almost as tall as a camel.

Cat, canary, and camel also begin with **C**.

Dd

Barkley is a dog. Dog begins with **D**.

Duck also begins with **D**.

Ee Ff

"Hey Ernie," called Payton Rose. "Your name begins with **E**. But you're not an animal!" laughed Payton Rose.

"Elephant begins with **E**. Snuffy has a long nose just like an elephant."

"Now, what animal begins with **F**?" thought Payton Rose. "Fox begins with **F**."

"A flying fox is another name for a bat. There's also flamingo, frog, and ferret."

Gg

"Elmo knows some animals beginning with **G**. There's a tall giraffe and tiny grasshopper. And don't forget Elmo's goldfish, Dorothy," said Elmo.

Hh

"That's a big animal with Zoe!" exclaimed Elmo.

"Yes. It has a very big name too," replied Zoe. "It's a hippopotamus."

Ii Jj

"What do you call those animals, Grover?" asked Payton Rose.

"An iguana is a type of lizard and has long spikes running down its back to its tail."

"The jaguar is a big spotted cat. And, do you know that an iguana and a jaguar both have long tails?" replied Grover.

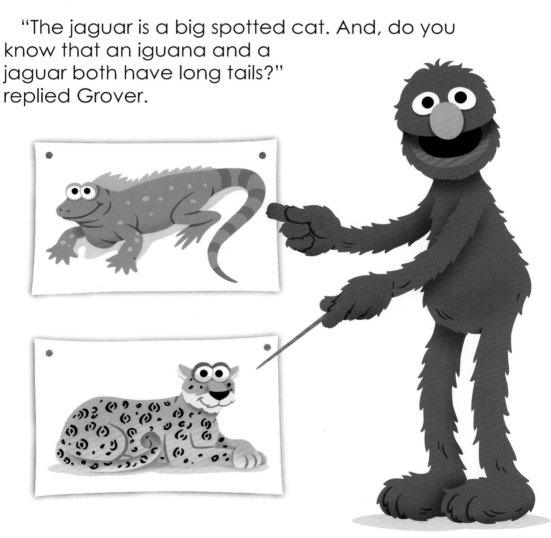

Kk

For animals beginning with **K**, we go to Australia, where we find kangaroo, koala, and kookaburra.

Ll

Llama, ladybug, and lizard all begin with **L**.

Mm

"Monkey begins with **M**. Look at Elmo playing with his monkey friends," laughed Payton Rose.

"Sometimes, Devyn, Dawson, Shaelyn and I pretend we are monkeys and swing from the branches of trees. It's a lot of fun!"

Nn Oo

Can you name Big Bird's feathered friends?

Nightingale begins with **N**. Did you know that nightingales also sing at night?

Owl begins with **O** and so does ostrich. An ostrich stands as tall as Big Bird.

Pp

Bert is playing with his pet pigeon, Bernice.

Pig begins with **P**, too.

Qq Rr

"I don't know any animals beginning with **Q**, do you Payton Rose?" asked Grover.

"Hmm, **Q** is a difficult letter, but I know that quail begins with **Q**!" replied Payton Rose.

"Of course! And there are lots of things beginning with **R**."

"There is rabbit, rat, reindeer, and rooster!" exclaimed Grover.

Ss

Zoe loves dancing with her animal friends beginning with **S**!

Swans glide elegantly across the water and bushy-tailed squirrels leap gracefully from tree to tree, just like a dancer.

Tt

Toucan begins with **T**. Toucans have large beaks and live in Central and South America.

Uu Vv

"Elmo, do you know any animals beginning with **U**?" asked Payton Rose.

"Elmo doesn't think there are any," replied Elmo.

"But there is the unicorn. The unicorn is a make-believe animal that looks like a horse with one horn," said Elmo.

"There aren't many animals beginning with **V** either," said Payton Rose. "Vulture begins with **V**."

Ww

Worm begins with **W**. Oscar loves worms!

What else begins with **W**? There is wallaby, walrus, and wolf. Can you name any others?

Xx

"There are two animals beginning with **X**!" exclaimed Grover.

"There is a xenopus which is a type of frog, and a bird called a xenops."

"Wow! Elmo never knew that before!" exclaimed Elmo.

Yy Zz

"We're almost through the alphabet. Can we find any animals beginning with **Y** and **Z**?" asked Payton Rose.

"Elmo knows! Yak begins with **Y**!" said Elmo excitedly.

"Yes, and there's a zebra. A zebra looks like a horse with black and white stripes," replied Payton Rose. "We've done it!"

"Now Elmo and Payton Rose can have even more fun learning our **ABCs**," giggled Elmo.

Super Letter Maze

Letters come in big and small sizes! The big partner is called uppercase. The small partner is called lowercase.

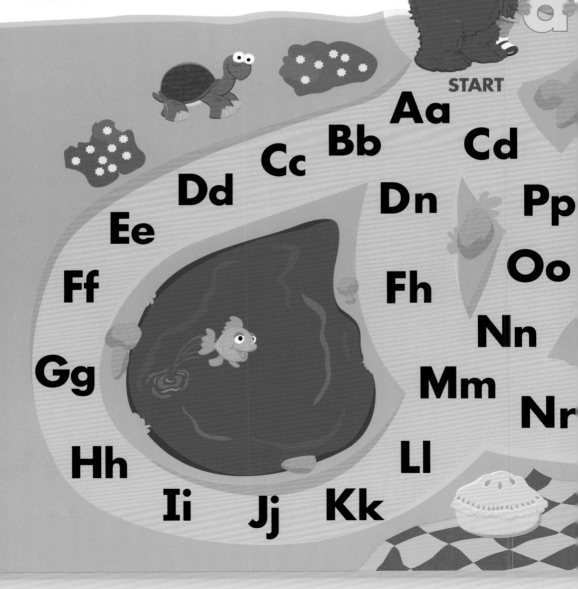

START

Aa Bb Cc Cd
Dd Dn Pp
Ee
Ff Fh Oo
Nn
Gg Mm Nr
Ll
Hh Ii Jj Kk

Help Cookie Monster and Prairie Dawn go from **Aa** to **Zz**. Draw a line through the path that shows letter partners.

Out to Sea

Payton Rose, say the name of each letter you see.
Then colour the spaces using the colour key.

Colour Key

A= B= C= D= E= F=

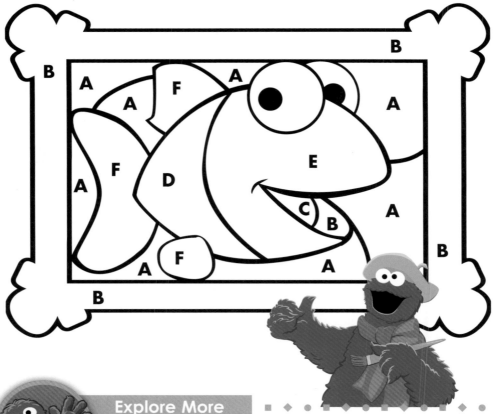

Explore More

Encourage your child to have fun writing letters. Sprinkle sand,
sugar, or powdered drink mix on a cookie sheet. Have your child
use his or her index finger to write **A, B, C, D, E,** and **F.**

Gg-Hh-Ii Hunt

Help Cookie Monster find the hidden letters.

First find and circle **G**, **H**, and **I**.
Then find and circle **g**, **h**, and **i**.

Monster Match-up

Payton Rose, help Cookie Monster match the cookies. Draw lines to match the cookies with their letter partners.

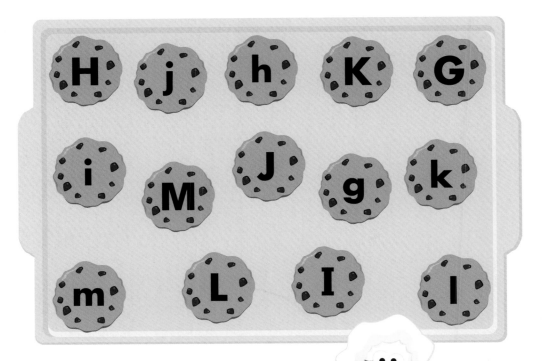

H   j   h   K   G

i   M   J   g   k

m   L   I   l

Explore More

Go through old newspapers with your child. Encourage your child to find examples of letter partners such as **M** and **m**. Cut out the letters and glue them onto a sheet of paper and make a letter collage.

Now on to Presents!

Help Cookie Monster match the presents.

Draw lines from each big present to the little presents that show its letter partner.

P N O

o n p o n

Finding Qq, Rr, and Ss

Payton Rose, help Cookie Monster find the letters hidden in the picture.

Look for big letters first!
Find and circle **Q**, **R**, and **S**.
Then find and circle **q**, **r**, and **s**.

Explore More

Help your child form letters with cold cooked spaghetti noodles. If you form the letters on wax paper, you can let them dry and harden. Then you can glue them on paper and paint them!

Move it!

Cookie Monster sees some moving vans.

Shade the wheel that has the letter partner on it.

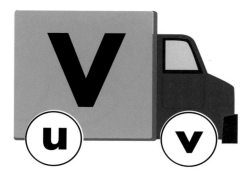

A Picture for You

Payton Rose, say the name of each letter you see. Then colour the spaces using the colour key.

Colour Key

W=   X=   Y=   Z=

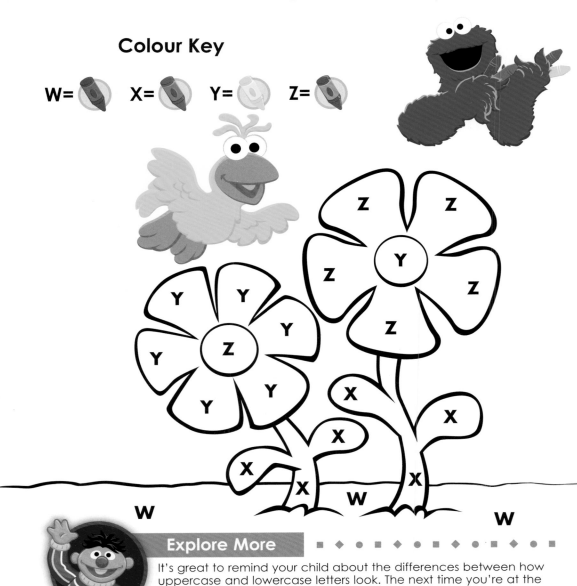

Get Your Party Hat

Big Bird and Snuffy are wearing party hats.

Circle all the party hats with uppercase letters.

Write the uppercase letter that your name begins with on this party hat.

A Big Letter Party

Payton Rose, come and join the party!

Colour all the balloons with uppercase letters.

 **Explore More** ◼ ◆ ● ◼ ● ◆ ◼ ● ◆ ● ◼

Help your child to name letters by playing a fun "Letter Alarm" game. Pretend you are sleeping and only "wake up" when your child calls out the letter you're "dreaming" about.

A Little Letter Party

Draw an **X** on all of the presents showing lowercase letters.

Play With Me

On a sheet of paper, write one uppercase or lowercase letter. Next to the letter, ask your child to write the matching letter partner. For example, if you write **T**, your child should write **t**, or if you write **b**, your child should write **B**. Repeat the activity for different letters.

A to Z Practice

Payton Rose, say the name of each picture.

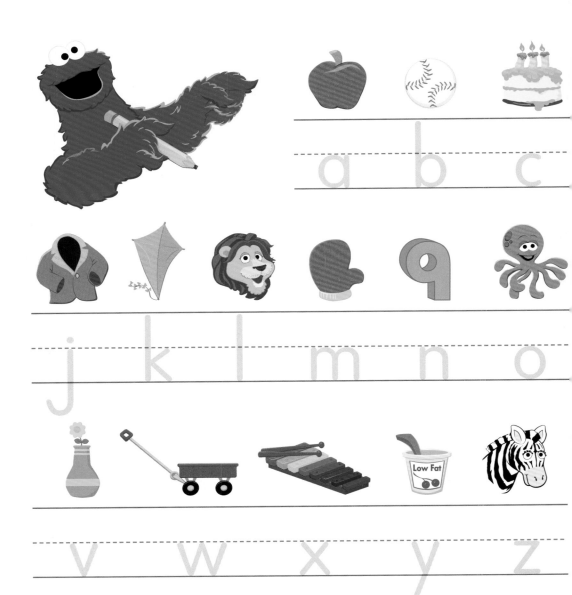

a   b   c

j   k   l   m   n   o

v   w   x   y   z

Then trace the letter.

d   e   f   g   h   i

p   q   r   s   t   u

Circle

■ ◆ ● ■ ◆ ● ■ ◆ ● ■ ◆ ● ■

Circle each picture whose name begins with **z**.

zebra   **Elmo**   **zero**

Time for Cake

It's September 1st so it must be Payton Rose's birthday! Cookie Monster has baked a cake for Payton Rose!

Colour all the cakes with lowercase letters, and then trace the lowercase letters in Happy Birthday.

b   L   Y   j

Q   e   D   w

H appy

B irthday

Payton Rose

Letter Champion

Cookie Monster has something special just for you!

Draw lines to connect the dots from **A** to **Z**. Then write your name on it.

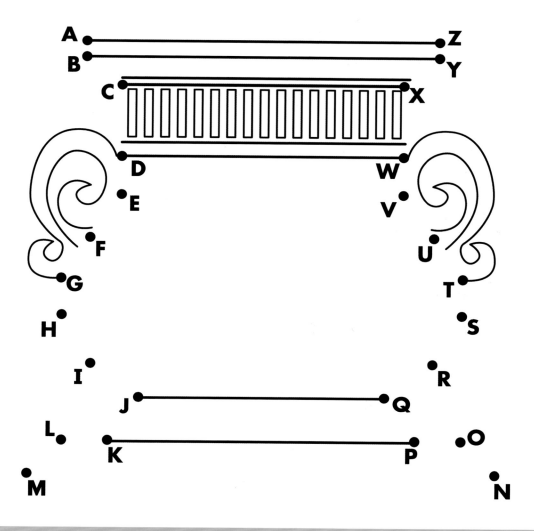

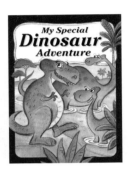

For our entire selection of books, please visit www.identitydirect.ca

This personalized Sesame Street ABCs book was especially created for
Payton Rose Johnson of Onoway with love from Grandma & Aunty Tabitha.

Additional books ordered may be mailed separately — please allow a few
days for differences in delivery times.

My Adventure Books

PO Box 6000
Brampton ON L6V 4N3
Phone: 905 840 4141
www.identitydirect.ca

0186 000402 0002 01 DM 0006

0 1 8 6 0 0 0 4 0 2 0 0 0 2 0 1